**Little Things I Love About You - Sister**

© 2019 Lil Big Hart

To:

_____

Message:

_____

_____

_____

Love from:

_____

1

You're awesome at

_____

**2**

When we were little you used to

_____

**3**

No matter what, you're always so

_____

**4**

Out of everybody in our family,
you're the one most likely to

_____

5

If it wasn't for you, I wouldn't

_____

6

I've always secretly admired your ability to

_____

7

You were cool when I borrowed your

_____

even though I

_____

8

I love that you still

_____

even though we're older now.

That face you pull when you're

_____

makes me

_____

10

The relationship you have with

_____

makes me so proud to be your sibling.

11

I will never get tired of your

_____

12

You're always there when I need

_____

13

You encourage me to

_____

14

You look so good when you wear your

_____

Can I borrow it someday? Maybe?

**15**

I LOVE that you love to

_____

16

You forgave me for

_____

17

You make me laugh when

_____

18

Wait. Do you still have my

_____

If so, now would be a good time
to give it back... while I'm in a good mood.

19

I love how you think I'm

_____

when I'm really not.

20

I'm so happy that you found

_____

21

Because of you I discovered a love of

_____

22

You put up with

_____

even though I know it annoys you.

23

The way you pretend to

_____

whenever I

_____

24

I love the way we always

_____

together.

25

Your

_____

is / are the best.

26

I'm so happy you no longer

_____

27

I can always be

_____

with you.

28

You taught me how to

_____

29

You're always willing to

_____

30

You're the only person who has seen me

_____

31

I love hearing your opinion on

_____

I love how you try to protect me from

_____

33

As much as I hate to admit it, you were right about

_____

You're the first person I think of when I

_____

35

You told me I was good at

_____

even though we both knew I sucked.

36

The times you helped me with

_____

even though I knew you didn't want to.

37

The way you patiently explain

_____

when I don't understand.

38

I love how you're always able to

_____

even in

_____

situations.

39

You are my

_____

40

You really know how to

_____

41

I love that we can talk for ages about

_____

I know I can rely on you to

_____

43

I love that you're willing to subject yourself to my

_____

44

Your dedication to

_____

inspires me.

45

My most favorite memory of you is

_____

46

The way you

_____

when we watch _____ together.

47

I love it when you share your

_____

with me.

48

I wish I had your

_____

49

I'm grateful to have you as my sister because

_____

50

I love how you're not afraid to

_____

51

The way you call me

_____

will never get old.

We have the best

_____

Made in United States
Troutdale, OR
12/05/2024